Abstract

Rule of Law in Mexico: Fact or Fiction?

To enhance the Rule of Law, Mexico has attempted to significantly change its entire system of laws, by moving towards a more transparent justice system, more akin to the open adversarial system possessed by the United States than the closed inquisitorial system employed for most of the 20th century in Mexico. Unfortunately, these constitutional, legislative and professional reforms made to the Mexican justice system, while a step in the right direction, have not yet yielded the desired effect of vastly improving the Rule of Law.

This paper will analyze key areas of the Mexican justice system and compare them to internationally accepted standards relating to the Rule of Law. Next, this paper will review recently enacted reforms to the Mexican justice system in order to determine whether these initiatives have had a significant effect on improving the system of justice in Mexico. Finally, this paper will make recommendations on the way ahead for Mexico in its journey to obtain stability through adherence to the Rule of Law. Ultimately, it is this paper's contention that the current efforts to reform Mexico's legal system have inadequately addressed the most significant issues relating to the establishment of a fair and just legal system in Mexico.

INTRODUCTION

The Mexican legal system's repeated failure to hold wrongdoers accountable for their actions, in an expeditious and equitable manner, communicates a socially dangerous message regarding the low level of risk associated with unlawful conduct.[1]

Mexico's increasingly tenuous domestic security situation, combined with the need to fulfill international treaty obligations demanding the rigorous implementation of the Rule of Law in both its criminal and commercial courts, have provided the impetus for the Government of Mexico to re-assess its archaic, corrupt, and woefully ineffective system of laws and regulations.[2] Recognizing that its track record of adherence to the principles of the Rule of Law are poorly perceived by both the international community and, more importantly, by its own citizens, the Mexican government's long term desire is to create a stronger, more independent, and more professional judiciary and justice system based upon the internationally understood definitions of the Rule of Law.[3]

Why should the government of Mexico care about the Rule of Law? Here are a few grim statistics that may have influenced the government: it is estimated that only 25% of all crimes in Mexico are actually reported to the police. Of these reported crimes, only 18% of these cases are actually investigated by law enforcement with less than 35% of these actual

---

[1] Robert Kossick, "The Rule of Law in Mexico," *Arizona Journal of International and Comparative Law* 21 (2004): 722-23; Kossick, *Rule of Law in Mexico*, 726; Alicia E. Yamin, and Ma. Pilar Noriega Garcia, "The Absence of the Rule of Law in Mexico: Diagnosis and Implications for a Mexican Transition to Democracy," 21 *Loyola of Los Angeles International & Comparative Int'l* (1999): 484.

[2] David A. Shirk, "Justice Reform in Mexico, Change & Challenges in the Judicial Sector," *Trans-Border Institute, Joan B. Kroc School of Peace Studies* (2010): 4, http://catcher.sandiego.edu/items/peacestudies/Shirk-Justice%20Reform%20in%20Mexico.pdf

[3] It requires, as well, measures to ensure adherence to the principles of supremacy of law, equality before the law, accountability to the law, fairness in the application of the law, separation of powers, participation in decision-making, legal certainty, avoidance of arbitrariness and procedural and legal transparency." Ibid.

investigations leading to effective prosecution in Mexican criminal courts.[4] Overall, roughly 1% of crimes committed in Mexico are ultimately brought to trial for prosecution and convictions secured.[5] Victims surveyed cite "waste of time" and "lack of trust" among key factors for not reporting crimes to the police.[6] Tellingly, Mexican police themselves "perceive a high degree of corruption on the force."[7] As a result of this stark inability to hold criminals, particularly violent members of the various drug cartels, accountable for crimes committed against its citizens, the domestic perception in Mexico is that criminals act with disturbing impunity.[8]

From a national security perspective, these statistics and perceptions matters a great deal to the Mexican government. If the average Mexican citizen does not trust the criminal justice system to pursue crime in a fair and open manner, the Mexican government stands little chance of gaining the support of the people in its attempt to suppress large-scale criminal behavior that is threatening to destabilize the Mexican regime. Ultimately, without an effective justice system representing their interests, a Mexican victim or witness who reports a crime runs a very serious risk of physical harm to themselves or their families if those crimes involve members of Mexican drug cartels.

This paper will analyze key areas of the Mexican justice system and compare them to internationally accepted standards relating to the Rule of Law. Next, this paper will review recently enacted reforms to the Mexican justice system in order to determine whether these initiatives have had a significant effect on improving the system of justice in Mexico. Finally,

---

[4] Shirk, *Justice Reform in Mexico*, 6.
[5] Ibid.
[6] Ibid., 5
[7] Ibid.
[8] United Nations General Assembly, *Report of the Special Rapporteur on the independence of judges and lawyers: Mission to Mexico*, 18 April 2011: 13. The United Nations has identified this perceived "impunity" as one of the major challenges facing Mexico's legal system.

this paper will make recommendations on the way ahead for Mexico in its journey to obtain stability through adherence to the Rule of Law. Ultimately, it is this paper's contention that the current efforts to reform Mexico's legal system have inadequately addressed the most significant issues relating to the establishment of a fair and just legal system in Mexico. As a result, in order to prevent further weakening of the social, political and economic fabric of Mexico, the government must double down on its efforts to reform the *entire* legal system or risk devastating long term consequences.

DISCUSSION

Mexico's System of Governance

Mexico has a constitutional government composed of executive, legislative and judicial branches.[9] While technically modeled after the United States' Constitution, the executive branch in Mexico has traditionally dominated both the legislative and judicial branches.[10] For example, more than 90% of all legislation is proposed by the executive rather than the legislative branch in Mexico; while the Mexican Congress, at the behest of the President, has amended the Mexican constitution over 369 times.[11] Similarly, the Mexican President has also traditionally exercised very close control over judicial appointments and judicial budgets, as well as tightly regulating the ability of the Mexican Supreme Court to declare legislation unconstitutional.[12] Thus, while it may appear that under the Mexican

---

[9] Mexican Constitution, Article 49
[10] Alex J. Gilman, "Making Amends with the Mexican Constitution: Reassessing the 1995 Judicial Reforms and Considering Prospects for Further Reform," *George Washington International Law Review* 35 (2003): 949
[11] Ibid, 950. 369 times between 1917-1984.
[12] Ibid

Constitution the three branches are co-equal members of government, the reality is that the Mexican judiciary has traditionally served as the weakest member of the three.[13]

Mexico's Legal System

Mexico's current legal system is based primarily upon the civil law inquisitorial system.[14] Under the inquisitorial or civil law system, the Mexican judiciary is exclusively guided in their decision-making by a complex and comprehensive series of legal codes and regulations that define all procedures and rights afforded to the Mexican citizenry.[15]

Under the Mexian civil law system, if a right or benefit is not defined in the criminal procedure code, it cannot be applied by the Mexican judiciary in a particular case.[16] Thus, unlike the common law doctrine of *Stare Decisis* used in the United States and Great Britain, there is no need for a Mexican judge to interpret statutes and regulations based upon the precedential value of historical cases. Rather than researching similarly situated cases, a Mexican judge simply has to look up the relevant regulation and in a formulaic manner -- apply it. Moreover, as a result of dealing exclusively with a minutely defined and detailed system of codes, Mexican judges are very inexperienced at identifying issues of a constitutional (or unconstitutional) nature. Obviously, this significant absence of initiative, coupled with the judiciary's complete reliance upon the legislature for exclusively enacting and amending laws, does not provide a basis for encouraging an independent judiciary.

---

[13] Shirk, *Justice Reform in Mexico*, 6.
[14] Gilman, *Making Amends*, 950.
[15] Ibid. Notably, these comprehensive codes are produced by the Mexican Congress with little input from the judiciary.
[16] Ibid.

Legal Education and Training

As a result of the civil law tradition in Mexico, neither the education or subsequent training of Mexican attorneys stress looking independently at the facts of a particular case within the context of a law. Rather, in Mexican law schools, in accordance with a method known as *Catedra Magistral* which is the rote memorization of codes, classifications and black letter laws are instead the norm.[17] Further, Mexican law school professors, unlike the majority of the legal faculty in the United States are considered adjunct faculty and are consequently poorly paid.[18] Furthermore, Mexican law professors are neither encouraged nor expected to add personal insight to lectures for their students.[19] In fact, it's not unusual for Mexican law professors to simply read the contents of an applicable code, regulation or article to their students instead of discussing the legal principles involved.[20]

In addition, despite the need, there are few practical internship programs available to law students that would enable them to receive invaluable experience and exposure to the chronically overburdened criminal justice system (not to mention the inherent benefits this would have for the poor who are unable to afford representation).[21]

Another important topic that currently receives scant attention or treatment is in the area of ethics and professional responsibility.[22] Unlike the United States, in Mexico's legal education system, for the majority of students, there are no mandatory requirements for

---

[17] Kossick, *Rule of Law in Mexico*, 731.
[18] Ibid., 737. "Consequently, many Mexican law schools have a difficult time attracting and/or retaining qualified and motivated professional educators and support staff."
[19] Ibid., 732
[20] Ibid.
[21] Ibid., 738. "Despite excessive levels of poverty, an under-staffed and under-funded public defender's office, and the essentially ineffective nature of the legal profession's approach to the provision of pro bono services, the overwhelming majority of Mexican law schools do not offer legal education for the mutual benefit of the poor and their students."
[22] Ibid., 739. There are no ramifications for student cheating or plagiarism, either. Many students "graduate" law schools without completing the thesis requirement. There are no bar exams certifying a basic competency level, either.

coursework on ethics or professional responsibility before attaining a degree.[23] In a country in which official corruption, particularly amongst law enforcement personnel, is viewed as a serious problem by the Mexican populace, having mandatory ethics training for law school students would seem to be a prudent move.

In addition to the lack of ethics training for law students, there are no mandatory continuing legal education requirements (CLE) in Mexico for practicing attorneys, as there are in the United States.[24] Consequently, Mexican attorneys have no obligation to keep abreast of changes in the law within their practice area – a potentially debilitating outcome in criminal or complex commercial cases. Practicing attorneys are also exempt from ethics or professional responsibility requirements.

The impact of this lack of supervision, training and accountability of attorneys can be far reaching. For example, if an attorney commits misconduct or negligence while representing a client in Mexico, a client has little legal recourse -- an ineffective assistance of counsel claim is currently not a legitimate cause of action in Mexican courts.[25] Not coincidentally, even if the courts were willing to hear such claims, there are no universal procedures for suspending or disbarring a Mexican attorney from the practice of law.[26]

Mexican Judiciary

In addition to having been subject to an inefficient and often inadequate system of legal education and training at law schools, Mexican attorneys who choose to become judges

---

[23] Kossick, *Rule of Law in Mexico*, 739.
[24] Ibid., 741.
[25] Alicia E. Yamin and Ma. Pilar Noriega Garcia, "The Absence of Rule of Law in Mexico: Diagnosis and Implications for a Mexican Transition to Democracy", *Loyola of Los Angeles International & Comparative Law Review* (1999): 512.
[26] UN Special Rapporteur, *Mexico*, 15

face other obstacles. In Mexico, due to the historical lack of judicial independence and overwhelming authority of the executive branch over the judiciary, judgeships, particularly at the state level, traditionally do not have the same level of prestige as in the United States.[27] Most judges are graduates of lowly regarded law schools. Moreover, Mexican judges are historically very poorly paid, and as a result, are very susceptible to corruption.[28] Additionally, for those judges that choose to hear cases involving corruption, human rights violations or involve members of Mexico's extremely violent drug cartels --personal safety, including the safety of family members, is a very significant issue that has been identified as a major problem by the United Nations.[29]

The Mexican government has recognized the importance of increasing the prestige of its judges (by significantly raising pay for federal judges and magistrates), by increasing the qualifications of sittings judges, as well as by toughening penalties for attacks on judicial officials. However, the brightest law school students from the top law schools in Mexico still choose to enter private practice instead of applying to the bench.

In sum, the majority of the current members of the Mexican judiciary are undertrained, poorly qualified or too susceptible to bribery and threats to sit as arbiters of justice. Simply put, the best and brightest lawyers in Mexico do not see the advantage in

---

[27] Kossick, *Rule of Law in Mexico*, 742. *See also* Yamin and Garcia, *Absence of the Rule of Law*, 494. "Numerous complaints about corruption, lack of independence and impartiality have made the judicial branch in Mexico one of the organs that enjoys the least public prestige. This mistrust is most pronounced with respect to the judicial branch at the state level, because of the influence which some individuals or groups exercise over the bodies responsible for the appointment of judges."
[28] Kossick, *Rule of Law in Mexico*, 742, 796. Pay reforms for Federal Judges and Magistrates have vastly increased salaries for the federal judiciary. Author also cites a UN study indicating that between _50-70%_ of the Mexican federal judiciary are corrupt (emphasis added).
[29] UN Special Rapporteur, *Mexico*, 13

becoming a judge. This is a major impediment to the advancement of the Rule of Law in Mexico.[30]

Right to a Fair Trial

The Mexican criminal trial under the traditional civil law setting, is an achingly slow, paper driven process that occurs in three unique stages: the preliminary hearing held by a public prosecutor, a more formal hearing phase involving the criminal court judge, prosecutor and defense attorney and finally, a conclusions stage where the judge considers all of the written and oral evidence and issues a verdict and sentence when applicable.[31] While the trials themselves are often public, much of the evidence is received by the court in the form of written affadavits and are submitted outside the public's presence. As a result of this paper driven process, in is not unsusual for cases to accumulate months or years of delays before a decision is rendered.[32]

To adhere to internationally mandated guidelines for criminal trials under Mexican law, the Mexican Constitution enumerates a number of personal rights and protections for Mexican citizens.[33] These constitutional and legislative protections include the right to a speedy trial, due process, the right to counsel, right against pre-trial confessions to the police, limited detention without charges, and the right to remain silent.[34] While these rights are clearly and unequivocably enunciated in the Mexican Constitiution, in practice, many of these rights are routinely sidestepped by the Mexican courts. [35]

---

[30] Kossick, *Rule of Law in Mexico*, 742.
[31] Yamin and Garcia, *Absence of the Rule of Law*, 482.
[32] Shirk, *Judicial Reform in Mexico*, 17.
[33] Mexican Constitution, Articles 13, 14, 16, 17, 19 and 20
[34] Mexican Constitution, Articles 13, 14, 16, 17, 19 and 20
[35] Yamin and Garcia, *Absence of the Rule of Law*, 482.

For example, during these three sets of hearings that comprise a Mexican criminal trial, the defendant has a right to counsel and to attend hearings held by the judge or prosecutor. However, in reality, the prosecutor and judge hold frequent hearings outside of the presence of the defendant, or their attorney, that often include taking testimony of critical government witnesses.[36] The public prosecutor – perhaps the most powerful player in the criminal justice systerm -- routinely submits uncontested documentary evidence directly to the trial judge. Additionally, government evidence is rarely turned over to the defendant prior to or during trial.[37] As a result, Mexican criminal defendants are routinely barred from effectively cross-examining or disputing the government's case at trial.

In addition, for indigent defendants, a public defender is appointed.[38] While appearing to satisfy international standards by giving indigent defenders access to public defenders, the public defender's offices in Mexico are overwhelmed with cases and are not sufficiently independent to act contrary to the more powerful public prosecutor's position in the court system.[39] For poor, indigenous, non-Spanish speaking defendants conditions are worse since translators are rarely available.[40]

Once arrested, many pre-trial defendants languish in severely overcrowded Mexican prisons for months and years before there case is heard – largely due to both the lack of a bail option in addition to the extensive bureaucratic delays associated with law enforcement.[41]

---

[36] Ibid., 483-4.
[37] Ibid., 484.
[38] Ibid., 483.
[39] Yarmin and Garcia, *Absence of the Rule of Law*, 483.
[40] Ibid.
[41] Ibid. Studies suggest that up to 50% of all prisoners in Mexico City were convicted of property crimes of less than $20.

Not surprisingly, a majority of those convicted are poor and did not have access to adequate legal counsel.[42]

Confessions

Confessions, regardless of how they are obtained, are traditionally considered by Mexican judges to be the most valuable type of admissible evidence used against a criminal defendant.[43] Despite having a constitutional amendment specifically prohibiting the use of confessions obtained by the police during the pre-trial investigation[44], Mexican judges give an inordinate amount of weight to confessions obtained during these same interrogations.[45] Moreover, the Mexican police have a long, sordid and well known history of extracting "confessions" using physical coercion.[46] In addition, as noted previously, while a right to counsel does exist at the pre-trial stage, attorneys are generally not present at these initial hearings to prevent police interrogations.[47] Thus, despite Mexican legislation introduced to outlaw both the use of torture and the banning of illegally obtained confessions -- use of these "confessions" remain routine in Mexican courts.[48] To compound this hypocritical practice, if torture allegations are made by a defendant in Mexico to a judge, the burden is on the defendant to prove that the government acted inappropriately. This is a difficult burden to surmount.[49]

Mexican Law Enforcement Agencies

---

[42] Shirk, *Judicial Reform in Mexico*, 7.
[43] Yamin and Garcia, *Absence of the Rule of Law*, 496.
[44] Mexican Constitution, Article 20, 1993 Amendment
[45] Yamin and Garcia, *Absence of the Rule of Law*, 497.
[46] United Nations, *Economic and Social Council, Commission on Human Rights, UN Special Rapporteur on Torture,* 1997, paragraph 78. As recently as 1997, torture has been described as a "frequent occurrence in many parts of Mexico."
[47] Yamin and Garcia, *Absence of the Rule of Law*, 483.
[48] Ibid., 496.
[49] Ibid., 498-9

The Mexican judiciary is not entirely at fault for the poor perception of the Mexican justice system. The various law enforcement agencies in Mexico are equally to blame. In Mexico, the police are are generally "poorly trained and inadequately equipped to employ modern investigative and forensic techniques in the course of a criminal proceeding."[50] Mexican law enforcement agencies are simply not trained to serve as active investigators or aggressive detectives[51]. Rather, the role of the police officer has traditionally been to serve as a visible deterrent to public crime[52]. As such, Mexican police are simply not trained to perform what is considered to be basic police work in the rest of the western world: collecting evidence, observing a proper chain of custody, dusting for fingerprints, etc. [53]

In addition to possessing a paucity of relevant modern training in police investigative work, state and federal law enforcement agencies have been found to "exhibit patterns of corruption and abuse."[54] Chillingly, police are blamed for a significant portion of violent crime.[55] Furthe, accusations that various law enforcement officials are involved with bribery and torture incidents against those arrested are all too common.[56]

Mexican Military as Law Enforcement

During the 1990s, in response to both the overall increase in the level of violence in Mexico, and the inability or unwillingness (i.e. rampant corruption) shown by local Mexican law enforcement agencies to combat rampant crime, the Mexican government deployed its professional military to handle many of the security issues that previously had been the

---

[50] Shirk, *Judicial Reform in Mexico*, 7
[51] Ibid., 7
[52] Ibid., 19
[53] Ibid., 19
[54] Ibid., 19
[55] Yamin and Garcia, *Absence of the Rule of Law*, 476
[56] Shirk, *Judicial Reform in Mexico*, 7

responsibility of local civilian law enforcement agencies.[57] The Mexican military's law enforcement mission was to fight drug cultivation and drug trafficking, mainly in northern Mexico.[58]

Unfortunately, while initially perceived as a prudent response to an immediate threat, the military's involvement in Mexico's traditional law enforcement anti-drug activities have subsequently drawn widespread international criticisms. This is largely due to the lack of appropriate training for law enforcement activities. The result has been documented human rights abuses, arbitrary detentions, disappearances and routine violations of victim's rights.[59] In addition, despite significant public criticism, the military, a powerful institution in Mexico, has been successful in systematically opposing calls for servicemembers accused of serious violations against civilians to be held accountable in civilian courts.[60]

Economic Impact

While the implications for possessing an antiquated and dysfunctional system of laws is fairly obvious on the Mexican criminal justice system, it also has significant repercussions on the economic front as well. The President of the Mexican Supreme Court recently stated, "confidence in the notion of justice, in judges, and in our laws is fundamental to Mexican and foreign investors' continued promotion of the country's economic development and generation of employment."[61] From an economic perspective, having a consistent and just legal system that abides by international laws and commercial treaties is vital to the

---

[57] Yamin and Garcia, *Absence of the Rule of Law*, 476
[58] Ibid.
[59] Ibid., 477
[60] Ibid., 480
[61] Robert M. Kossick, "The Enforcement of Local Judgments in Mexico: An Analysis of the Quantitative & Qualitative Perceptions of the Judiciary & Legal Professions," *University of Miami Inter-American Law Review* 34 (2003): 456

continued economic viability of the Mexican nation. In a world of increasing complexity, Mexico is a signatory to numerous international trade pacts, and other commercial treaties, that require the Mexican justice system to fairly adjudicate international and domestic commercial disputes and claims in domestic courts.[62]

Unfortunately, Mexico's commercial laws and regulations are perceived as "outdated" and "unclear" by many international corporations that do business or want to do business in Mexico.[63] The Mexican commercial court process that adjudicates such claims are similarly considered to be of "interminable" length and do not have a strong reputation for enforcing compliance.[64] Without serious reformation of its commercial courts and fair adherence to laws governing commercial transactions, international corporations are less likely to invest directly in the economic infrastructure of Mexico. This is an outcome that is diametrically opposed to the strategy to increase both exports and foreign investment within Mexico.[65]

Attempts at Reformation

In December 1994, President Zedillo, was able to push through a series of reforms that restructured the federal judiciary in an attempt to create more independence and transparency in the judicial branch of the Federal government, as well as to increase the professionalism and efficiency of the Mexican court system.[66] By virtue of this legislation, a Federal Judicial Council (FJC) was specifically created to relieve the Mexican Supreme

---

[62] Kossick, *Rule of Law in Mexico*, 726.
[63] Ibid., 720
[64] Ibid., 720
[65] Ibid., 720
[66] Shirk, *Judicial Reform in Mexico*, 11. It was hoped that this would relieve a tremendous backlog in cases throughout the court system.

15

Court of its administrative and personnel decision-making authority.The FJC was expected to assume these responsibilities in order to allow the Mexican Supreme Court to become more independent minded and to focus its attention on substantive court and constitutional issues.[67]

Probably the most important piece of the 1994 legislation was the impact these laws had on the composition, independence and authority of the Mexican Supreme Court. The 1994 reforms reduced the number of judges on the Supreme Court from twenty-one to eleven, while sharply limiting partisan politics during the selection process by increasing approval majority of the Senate to 2/3 of all votes.[68] Additionally, under this groundbreaking new law, the Mexican executive and legislative branches, for the first time, gave the Supreme Court some authority to declare legislation or other government actions unconstitutional.[69] Though the authority to pursue one of these *acciones de inconstitucionalidad* was limited to key government officials, this was new territory for the Supreme Court and significantly increased their independence from the other two branches of government.[70]

While the 1994 reforms were an important and groundbreaking series of attempts to reform the Mexican judicial system, the subsequent 2008 constitutional and legislative reforms were much more substantive. Under the 2008 reforms, for the first time, actual substantive changes were made to the Mexican civil law trial system – a system that had been in use by Mexico for well over a century. Under the 2008 laws, new advsersarial procedures were introduced in state and federal courts in order to move away from the closed, paper-

---

[67] Kossick, *Rule of Law in Mexico*, 755
[68] Yamin and Garcia, *Absence of the Rule of Law*, 501-2
[69] Shirk, *Judicial Reform*, 11
[70] Ibid., 11

driven evidenciary process and towards a set of judicial hearings focused on oral advocacy, openness and a much more efficient and timely process.[71]

Additionally, to more effiiciently address the tremendous number of pending cases in the justice system (a byproduct of which resulted in severe prison overcrowding), alternative sentencing in the form of plea bargaining and alternative disupte resolutions (ADR) were introduced.[72]

Another key reform introduced in 2008 involved strengthening the rights of the accused, particularly as they related to due process and the right to a speedy trial. New reforms limited the time that defendants could be held in jail for minor offenses and introduced bail requirements for non-violent offenses.[73] The laws requiring professional legal representation throughout the legal process were also strengthened.[74]

In attempting to remedy the very real professionalism and competency issues of the Mexican police, the 2008 law attempted to affect a huge sea change by requiring Mexican law enforcement agencies to officially include a much "greater integration in the administration of justice."[75] For the first time, Mexian police were now required to develop the ability and skills to investigate crimes and professionally gather evidence in order to properly assist Mexican prosecutors and judges in adjudicating cases.[76]

Critique of the Reforms

---

[71] Ibid., 12
[72] Shirk, *Judicial Reform in Mexico*, 13
[73] Ibid., 17.
[74] Ibid.
[75] Mexican Constitution, Article 21, Paragraph 1 (1917)
[76] Shirk, *Judicial Reform in Mexico*, 19. "As many as 75% of Mexico's more than 400,000 police lacked investigative capacity, were deployed primarily for patrol and crime prevention, and were largely absolved of responsibilities to protect or gather evidence."

In reviewing these changes to Mexican law, there appears to be a wide disparity between the appearance of a comprehensive reformation of the administration of justice system and the actual implementation and practice of these new rules and regulations, that occur on a day-to-day basis. For example, despite a federal law mandating these comprehensive changes to the civil law trial system in all states and the federal government over a period of eight years, only 13 of 32 states have implemented these changes.[77] Recognizing Mexico's glacial pace, critics continue to complain that Mexico has been unable or unwilling to act upon the 2008 constitutional reforms with any urgency.[78]

Also, it is not yet clear whether Mexico is willing (or has the monies available) to invest the huge resources necessary to pay for the required training, education and modernization of the 400,000 person Mexican police. Without these critical investments, the reforms will have a difficult chance to succeed. Furthermore, while the changes to strengthen due process rights, including the right to adequate counsel and a speedy trial were targeted to address very real weaknesses in the criminal justice system, they are the veritable toothless tiger when considering that the entire mexican legal education system needs to be rebuilt. Simply increasing the pay of the judges, while helpful, is not the answer.

In other words, Mexico simply cannot expect to have modern courts in which well trained and well paid judges are neutral arbiters of justice, in an adversarial system when they lack fundamental legal education on such topics as professional ethics, constitutional rights, human rights and trial advocacy. In a similar vein, while it is important to strengthen the requirement for professional representation of all defendants, the Mexican legal system

---

[77] Ibid., 3. See also Malkin, Elisabeth, "Mexican justice in the dock; A wrongfully jailed man becomes a symbol of the legal system's failings." *The International Herald Tribune*, March 7, 2011, Pg. 2.
As of April 2011, Mexico City, the largest metropolitan area in Mexico has not yet completed these reforms.
[78] *Los Angeles Times*, Editorial, "Mexico's Weak Rule of Law," April 18, 2011, sec. A., http://articles.latimes.com/2011/apr/18/opinion/la-ed-graves-20110418

cannot provide "professional" representation without an adequate nationwide legal quasi-official governming system, composed of attorneys that can certify, supervise and discipline all attorneys in Mexico (i.e. a Mexican bar association, implementation of a national bar examination, standing ethics committees, etc.). Unfortunately, reforms to date fail to address these critical issues.

Finally, any substantial or procedural reforms to the judicial system in Mexico are meaningless without also addressing the corruption and human rights issues. Mexico has one of the most corrupt systems of law in the western hemisphere.[79] As addressed earlier in this paper, Mexican police officials and judges are routinely accused of corruption and abuse. There is no indication that these practices have changed.

Proponents of the recent reforms argue that the scope and extent of the changes to the Mexican justice system are generally headed in the right direction and should be given time to percolate in order to create a stronger system of Rule of Law. After all, the argument goes, Mexico has had these problems for well over a century. A change that strengthens the Rule of Law is positive change. However, since 2008, the impunity through which well organized drug cartels have attacked both the infrastructure of Mexico and its citizens has risen considerably. Futher, the domestic perception of the Mexican justice system is not improving. Mexico does not have the luxury of taking a wait and see approach when considering whether these changes are "enough."

---

[79] Agrast, M.D. et al., *Rule of Law Index*, World Justice Project, 2011: 26-7, http://worldjusticeproject.org/rule-of-law-index/ Mexico ranks 11th out of 12 surveyed countries in the western hemisphere for criminal justice system (64/66 globally) and 10th out of 12 countries surveyed in the western hemisphere for corruption (53/66 globally).

CONCLUSIONS/RECOMMENDATIONS

In confronting the lack of transparency and effectiveness in its criminal justice system by launching a series of reforms, it appears that the long-term desire of the Mexican government is to overcome the instability posed by powerful domestic drug trafficking cartels, by creating an environment in which crimes can be effectively investigated, criminals promptly arrested, and convictions fairly pursued in criminal courts in a transparent and effective manner. In that light, multiple Mexican governments have pursued major reformations of the criminal justice system with the hope that an implementation of an effective system of laws will create goodwill and trust amongst the domestic populace for critical public institutions such as the police, prosecutors and the courts -- while striving to counter-balance and ultimately diminish the chaos caused by powerful domestic criminal cartels within Mexico.

These reforms have met with limited success so far. The reformation of the Supreme Court and the introduction of the FJC have given the judicial branch of the Mexican government far more independence than it had previously achieved. However, the Mexican legal system writ large is still rife with allegations of human rights abuse, corruption, and professional incompetence – all issues that can be in part linked to the lack of a competent professional legal education and training system in Mexico. All parties to the Rule of Law system in Mexico must be given adequate training, pay and education for the legal system to be rehabilitated at or near international standards. Until the Mexican legal education system is overhauled from the bottom up, to include: 1) the hiring of professionally competent instructors; 2) requiring the teaching of relevant legal educational topics incorporating rigid graduation requirements; and 3) continuing legal education requirements that mandate a basic level of competency and ethical conduct both during and after graduation, these reforms will be difficult to achieve.

To avoid a complete breakdown of confidence in the Mexican government – a potentially disastrous situation for its all its neighbors, the United States must significantly increase direct and indirect support to Mexico through public and private programs that specifically enhance Mexico's legal education and training system; properly equip, train and educate both the Mexican law enforcement agencies and military units performing the same law enforcement functions; and provide much needed expertise to the Mexican government on a more complete reformation of the current Mexican legal system -- to include the implementation of a nationwide system of supervision for Mexican attorneys, judges and court personnel. Until the legal education system has fixed its fundamental flaws and the perception of the legal system is rehabilitated, there will be few significant changes to the view of the average Mexican citizen that the Mexican court system is thoroughly corrupt, incompetent and biased in favor of the those with the resources to manipulate it.

BIBLIOGRAPHY

Archibold, Randal C., "Clinton Voices U.S. Support of Mexico in Trip." *New York Times*, January 25, 2011, sec. A.

Agrast, M.D. et al., *Rule of Law Index*, World Justice Project, 2011, http://worldjusticeproject.org/rule-of-law-index/

Cooper, James, "Legal reform, not gun battles, for Mexico." *Providence Journal-Bulletin*, January 27, 2011, Pg. 7.

Gilman, A.J., "Making Amends with the Mexican Constitution: Reassessing the 1995 Judicial Reforms and Considering Prospects for Further Reform," *George Washington International Law Review* 35 (2003)

Kossick, Robert M., "The Rule of Law in Mexico," *Arizona Journal of International and Comparative Law* 21 (2004)

Kossick, Robert M., "The Enforcement of Local Judgments in Mexico: An Analysis of the Quantitative & Qualitative Perceptions of the Judiciary & Legal Professions," *University of Miami Inter-American Law Review* 34 (2003)

Los Angeles Times, Editorial, "Mexico's Weak Rule of Law." April 18, 2011, sec. A., http://articles.latimes.com/2011/apr/18/opinion/la-ed-graves-20110418

Malkin, Elisabeth, "Mexican justice in the dock; A wrongfully jailed man becomes a symbol of the legal system's failings." *The International Herald Tribune*, March 7, 2011, Pg. 2.

Mexican Constitution (1917)

Miroff, Nick, "Tough cop for a tough town." *The Washington Post*, July 25, 2011, sec. A.

Nieto, Enrique P., "A four-pronged strategy to reduce violence in Mexico." *Financial Times* (London, England), January 7, 2011, Pg. 8

Roig-Franzia, Manuel, "A former foreign minister diagnoses Mexico's national malady." *The Washington Post*, June 26, 2011, sec. B.

Salas, G. R., "Guidelines to Reform Mexican Criminal Procedure," *Southwestern Journal of Law and Trade in the Americas* 15 (2008)

Shirk, D.A., "Justice Reform in Mexico, Change & Challenges in the Judicial Sector," *Trans-*

Border Institute, Joan B. Kroc School of Peace Studies (2010*)*: 4,
http://catcher.sandiego.edu/items/peacestudies/Shirk-
Justice%20Reform%20in%20Mexico.pdf

United Nations, *Report of the Secretary-General: The rule of law and transitional justice in conflict and post-conflict societies,* 2004
http://www.unrol.org/article.aspx?article_id=3

United Nations General Assembly, *Report of the Special Rapporteur on the independence of judges and lawyers: Mission to Mexico*, 18 April 2011

Yamin, A.E. and Garcia, P. N., "The Absence of the Rule of Law in Mexico: Diagnosis and Implications for a Mexican Transition to Democracy," 21 *Loyola of Los Angeles International & Comparative Int'l* (1999)